Ludwig van Beethoven

COMPLETE
PIANO SONATAS

Ludwig van Beethoven

COMPLETE
PIANO SONATAS

Edited by

HEINRICH SCHENKER

with a new introduction by

CARL SCHACHTER

IN TWO VOLUMES
VOLUME I
(Nos. 1 - 15)

DOVER PUBLICATIONS, INC.

NEW YORK

This Dover edition, first published in 1975, is an unabridged and corrected republication of *L. van Beethoven / Klaviersonaten / Nach den Autographen und Erstdrucken rekonstruiert von Heinrich Schenker*, originally published in four volumes by Universal-Edition A. G., Vienna and Leipzig, ca. 1923.

The footnotes have been translated, and Schenker's preface retranslated, specially for the present edition, which also includes a new introduction by Carl Schachter.

The publisher is grateful to Miss Marie Powers for lending copies of the original for reproduction. A number of corrections have been introduced tacitly into the text of the present edition.

International Standard Book Number: 0-486-23134-8
Library of Congress Catalog Card Number: 74-83473

Manufactured in the United States of America
Dover Publications, Inc.
180 Varick Street
New York, N.Y. 10014

Introduction to the Dover Edition

For a hundred and fifty years the thirty-two piano sonatas of Beethoven have formed a cornerstone of the pianist's repertory. Although other composers—especially Haydn and Mozart—have written magnificent piano sonatas, the thirty-two of Beethoven surely contain the supreme examples of the classical solo sonata. One might imagine that works so universally loved and admired would always have been available in accurate and authoritative editions. As it happens, however, almost the very opposite is true. The edition reprinted here is the first that comes close to being an exemplary one. Not only is it a remarkable achievement in itself, but also it marks a watershed in music scholarship and editorial practice. The editor, Heinrich Schenker (1868–1935), is best known today as a music theorist whose contributions are generally regarded—even by those who do not subscribe to them—as among the most significant in the entire history of tonal music.[1]

Schenker, however, was much more than a theorist. To brilliant and original thinking his work unites scrupulous, painstaking scholarship and profound artistic vision. In other words Schenker's work brings together the activities usually carried on separately by theorists, musicologists and interpretative musicians. In uniting these activities (to the benefit of all of them), Schenker's work is unique in the history of musical scholarship and thought.

At the time this edition first appeared most pianists, teachers and students used one of a number of "practical" or "performing" editions whose editors thought nothing of changing or adding to the composer's marks for dynamics, phrasing, articulation, and indeed even the notes themselves if they felt impelled to do so. Some of these editions are still in print and are occasionally used by the provincial or igno-

rant. Besides these corrupt texts two more serious editions were available, at least in libraries, but were much less widely used. These were the volumes of piano sonatas from the Beethoven *Gesamtausgabe* (published by Breitkopf and Härtel in the 1860's) and the so-called *Urtext* edition (also Breitkopf, 1898). Both have been reprinted and the latter is widely used today—indeed probably more widely used than when it was one of the only two editions that could be taken at all seriously. Although it is vastly superior to the "practical" editions its shortcomings are many, largely owing to the fact that the editor (Carl Krebs) did not use as sources more than a very few of the available autographs (he did *not* use Opp. 53, 57, 79, 90, 109, 110 or 111; he did use Opp. 78, 81a and 101).

Schenker's edition began to appear in single sonatas in the early 1920's; by 1923 the complete set was available in four volumes. Before producing this edition of all the sonatas, Schenker had brought out annotated editions (*Erläuterungsausgaben*) of four of the last five sonatas (Opp. 101, 109, 110 and 111). These appeared between 1913 (Op. 109) and 1920 (Op. 101) and contained exemplary reproductions of Beethoven's texts together with highly detailed commentaries including information on the source materials (autographs, first editions, corrected copies), interpretations of Beethoven's sketches where these were available, analyses of form and structure (the edition of Op. 101 contained Schenker's first published attempts at graphic analysis), suggestions for interpretation, and an exhaustive critique of other editions and of the important literature about each sonata. It would be safe to say that no masterpieces of music had ever received such detailed and loving treatment from an editor before; and indeed these

---

[1] Schenker's *Five Graphic Music Analyses* (*Fünf Urlinie-Tafeln*) is available with a new introduction by Felix Salzer (New York: Dover Publications, 1969). Salzer's own *Structural Hearing* is based upon Schenker's approach (New York: Dover Publications, 1962). The only book-length work of Schenker's available in English is his *Harmony* (ed. Oswald Jonas, Chicago: University of Chicago Press, 1954). Translations of articles by Schenker have appeared in the *Journal of Music Theory* and *The Music Forum*.

annotated editions mark the beginning of much that is best in modern editorial practice.[2] Schenker was the first to make a truly critical edition and to develop and describe principles of editorship.

Perhaps the most important of these principles was to regard the autograph as the primary evidence of the composer's intention unless there were valid reasons to the contrary.[3] Schenker used more autographs as sources than had any previous editor of the sonatas; specifically he used Opp. 26, 27 No. 2, 28, 57, 78, 81a (first movement), 101, 109, 110 (both autographs) and 111 (both autographs). He did not have access to the autographs of Opp. 53, 79 and 90, which have been used by some later editors; the autographs of the early sonatas and of Op. 106 have long since disappeared. Schenker also consulted first editions and copies corrected by Beethoven.

The way in which Schenker used this material set an entirely new trend. He was the first consciously to reproduce, as far as it is possible in print, the visual impression of the autograph. In other words he tried to be faithful not only to the contents of the works but also to the form in which the autograph presents them to the eye of the viewer. Very often Beethoven writes in a manner contrary to standard notational practice. Most editors before Schenker simply "corrected" these irregularities without realizing that they were possibly blocking access to an understanding of the composition. Conventionally, for example, the upper stave in piano music is mostly assigned to the right hand, and the lower to the left. How much more expressive is Beethoven's notation at the beginning of the last movement of Op. 27 No. 2, where the right-hand part emerges out of the lower stave into the light of day. This beautiful notation was not reproduced in earlier critical editions nor, indeed, in all later ones (for example, Artur Schnabel's). In the first movement of Op. 101, bar 16, the left-hand part (e^1–$f\sharp^1$–$g\sharp^1$) grows out of the chordal third e^1–$g\sharp^1$ just played by the right hand. By placing the left-hand part in the upper stave, Beethoven shows this important connection.

Another standard notational practice is stemming notes down in the upper part of the stave and up in the lower part. Beethoven sometimes writes his stems contrary to rule with great expressive effect. In Op. 111, first movement, bars 64–65, Beethoven stems the right-hand part up although it is in an extremely high register. In so doing he makes it stand out as a separate voice from the repetition of the same figure an octave lower (bars 65–66), and conveys an impression of orchestral writing. This beautiful notation comes from the Bonn autograph, not the Berlin one which has been reproduced in facsimile. Schenker selected it because of its superior expressive power. Other instances of irregular stemming are: again Op. 111, first movement,

bars 36–39, right-hand part stemmed down to show that it is a middle voice; Op. 109, second movement, bars 70–71, and third movement, Var. IV, bar 1, right-hand part stemmed down for the same reason; Op. 101, last movement, beginning of fugato (bars 124–129), left-hand part stemmed down to emphasize bass register. A more subtle stemming appears in the Arietta of Op. 111, bar 11, where the right-hand thirds are stemmed up as if to emphasize the great distance separating them from the lower parts.

Sometimes Beethoven does not use beams in the usual way. An astonishing notation occurs in the Variation movement of Op. 111, bar 59, where all the notes in the bar are grouped on a single beam as if to counteract any tendency to emphasize single beats (in the same variation also see the right-hand part of bar 64, *prima volta*). Another unusual case in Op. 111: breaking the right-hand beam before the last sixteenth note of bar 110, first movement; its purpose is to point up the change in register. This last notation seems not to be followed in any other edition.

Beethoven's use of slurs sometimes emphasizes the polyphonic character of a passage. See the Rondo of Op. 28, bars 95–99, where the right-hand part is slurred over the bar while the left-hand slur stops before the bar line. A similar use of slurs will be found in the Adagio of Op. 31 No. 2, last four bars. Again, most available editions have not followed Beethoven's intentions faithfully.

Op. 110 contains a number of details which are incorrect in most other editions. In the first movement, bars 13 and 15, staccato signs should occur only at every quarter-beat rather than at every eighth as in bars 12 and 14. The pedal markings in the Trio of the Scherzo should come at the beginning of bars 48, 56, etc., rather than on the second beat. In the Recitativo of the last movement (bar 5) Schenker's reading of the repeated $a\natural^2$ follows the Bonn autograph; Schenker's reasons for adopting this reading are given in a fascinating rhythmic analysis of the passage in the annotated edition of the sonata mentioned earlier in this Introduction. One final point: the title of the second fugue, bars 136 ff., is given by Schenker in two lines, thus indicating that *poi a poi di nuovo vivente* refers not merely to a gradual quickening of the tempo (despite Schnabel's assertion to the contrary), but to an ever increasing animation in the composition itself.

The decision to adopt a given reading can be difficult, especially if there is more than one source (as in the Recitativo of Op. 110), if the source is unclear, or if the primary source—the autograph—has disappeared. Such decisions require superior musical insight and cannot be arrived at on purely philological grounds. An instance of this occurs at the end of the development section of the first movement of Op. 106, bars 224 (last eighth) to 226; should it read $A\sharp$ or $A\natural$? The autograph has disappeared and the

---

[2] These annotated editions have not been translated into English. They have been reissued in revised form in the original German as Beethoven, *Die letzten Sonaten*, Erläuterungsausgabe von Heinrich Schenker, herausgegeben von Oswald Jonas (Vienna: Universal-Edition, 1971–72).

[3] Schenker was the first to emphasize the importance of autographs and was instrumental in the founding of the Photogramm-Archiv of the Austrian National Library, the first photocopy archive of musical autographs.

Page 10 of the first Viennese edition of Op. 106, including the disputed passage discussed in the text. (Reproduced from a copy formerly in the possession of Heinrich Schenker.)

only sources are two inaccurate first editions—particularly inaccurate, as it happens, on this very page.[4] At this point in the composition there is a key signature of five sharps; the first editions do not supply a natural sign. On grounds of voice leading and harmonic implication, however, Schenker sides with those who believe that the editions are faulty and that the natural is required. The reasons for this decision are too complex to go into here (and Schenker's footnote does not provide a complete explanation). Furthermore, any interpretation of such a passage, however well founded, remains ultimately unverifiable. But surely no previous editor had approached this problem with the knowledge and capacity for musical thinking that Schenker had and it is doubtful, to say the least, that any future editor will do so.

A problem of a different kind occurs at the second theme of the first movement of Op. 57, bars 35 ff. The autograph survives but the notation of the slurs is inconsistent and in a way that does not suggest a purposeful variation. Here again the editor's musical insight must point the way to a solution. In the version that Schenker chooses, the first two tones (C and E♭) are slurred separately from the continuation of the melody. This highlights a significant aspect of the theme: that the opening upbeat consists of the same two tones as the end of the phrase (bar 39). Again this beautiful articulation occurs, as far as we know, in no other edition.

Another most unusual and valuable feature of this edition is the *fingerings*. It is not generally known that Schenker was a practical musician as well as a theorist and scholar; in his early years he was active as a composer and pianist. His personal copies of music abound with pencilled-in interpretation marks dealing with dynamics, agogics, rubato and (in piano music) fingerings, pedal and so forth. This edition, of course, contains no interpretative supplements to the score, for Schenker wished to avoid anything that would obscure Beethoven's text. However, the very detailed fingerings, properly understood, provide many clues to interpretation.

One might say that piano fingerings tend to follow one or another of two principles. The first is to make the passage as easy as possible technically; the second is to create a physical gesture that will help to achieve a desired musical result (e.g., shading, articulation or timing). These principles are not mutually exclusive. Most sensitive pianists will follow both in working out the fingerings for a composition, and fingerings of both types are found in this edition. However, too great a reliance on the first approach carries with it the danger of separating the execution of the notes from that of the interpretative nuances; shadings and articulations are superimposed by an act of will on a stereotyped and undifferentiated physical pattern. The most interesting of Schenker's fingerings are those of the second type—not just "basic" fingerings that "work" technically but ones

that help to express compositional ideas in playing. There are more of these in Schenker's edition than in any other and a great deal of insight into the music can be gained from a thoughtful study of these fingerings. We shall point to a few of these arranged by category.

Motivic: Op. 81a, I, Introduction, bars 9–11 in the left hand. The basic "farewell" motive of a descending third is introduced in descending sequence in the bass. Schenker maintains a parallel fingering (3-4-5) for each statement of the figure and secures a legato by switching fingers on the same key. In the Allegro of the same movement, bars 39–41, the tenor part (left hand) plays a development of this same basic motive (C–D–E♭–D–C). Schenker's fingering (2-1-2-1-2) helps us to bring out the tenor part. The same motive (E♭–D–C) recurs in bars 48–49, l. h. (with chromatic passing tone), and in bar 61 in rhythmic diminution. Here again the fingerings help to project this figure.

Rhythmic and melodic grouping: A remarkable fingering occurs throughout the Trio of Op. 110, II (bars 41–95). The rhythmic texture—continuous eighths in the right hand, off-beat quarters in the left—makes it very difficult for the player to express the inner groupings of the eight-bar phrases. By placing the fifth finger at the head of each group (2 plus 2 plus 4 bars), Schenker helps the player to clarify the melodic and rhythmic contour of the phrases. In Op. 31 No. 1, II, bars 14–15, the fingering—in particular the upper fingering—follows the melodic-rhythmic grouping of the right-hand part (groups of two, four and three tones). In Op. 109, Prestissimo, bars 170 ff., the use of the thumb in the left-hand part facilitates an emphasis on the chordal tones on the first beats.

Sliding: Schenker suggests sliding with one finger onto an adjacent key for various musical reasons. In Op. 31 No. 2, I, bar 141, the sliding 5-5 produces a slackening of motion for the melodic progression B♭–A. In Op. 101, Adagio, bar 1 and especially bar 4, the sliding 2-2 creates a languid, "tired" expression. In the presto passage immediately before the final Allegro of the same sonata, the sliding of the fourth finger is to ensure the sounding, through the diminuendo, of the chordal seventh D♮.

Silent change of finger on one key: The switching of fingers occurs mostly, of course, to secure legato. Thus in Op. 22, Adagio, bars 2 and 5, the changing of fingers helps to connect the appoggiaturas to their resolutions and to the remaining tones of these bars, which continue without a break from the resolutions. In the Andante espressivo of Op. 81a, bar 15, however, the change from 1 to 2 is not only for legato but also to bring out the tension and release of the syncopated melodic line; the player ought to make the change at the middle of the bar so that he "feels" the suppressed beat. (The Henle edition, incidentally, has a single slur over the entire bar, a "modernizing" of Beethoven's notation that serves neither him nor the performer.)

---

[4] We have reproduced the page in question from the first Viennese edition (Artaria 1819). The reader will note that there are many necessary accidentals missing from the page (bar 222, ♮ for the last G; bar 237, ♭ for the a^2; bar 239, ♭ for the first a^2). And

in particular note that the rhythm of the right-hand part in the disputed passage itself (bars 224–226) is wrong. The autograph was probably very hard to decipher.

Also for the sake of syncopation: the repeated two-note figure g^1–$f\sharp^1$ at the end of the exposition of Op. 90, I (bars 75–77). Sometimes switching fingers produces an agogic nuance by making the hand linger on a key. Such is the case in Op. 79, II, bar 10, where changing from 1 to 2 draws out the first of the two slurred tones and simulates a vocal *portamento*. A similar vocal effect—perhaps even more beautiful—is produced by changing from 4 to 5 on the eighth-note b^1 in the Rondo of Op. 10 No. 3, bar 6. In the Rondo of Op. 7, bars 161–162, an almost extravagant change (4-5-4 on the same key) helps the player to bring out the *ffp* and, by a slight hesitation, to signal the return to E♭ major after a brief but most unexpected departure from it.

Articulation: Many of Schenker's fingerings are designed to produce a desired articulation. In the Adagio of Op. 31 No. 2, bar 2, the right-hand part is fingered 2-3-5 to provide a closer physical connection between the first two notes, which are slurred together, than between the second and third. (Schnabel gives the same fingering, but changes the slur so that it covers all three notes.) In Variation I of the last movement of Op. 109, bar 15, the fingering ensures the necessary separation between the two-note groups.

Pianistic: Schenker's fingerings are primarily intended to bring out musical ideas but many of them are also helpful technically. Among these are: his suggestion for the *Waldstein* trill (Op. 53, III, bars 485 ff.); the thirty-second-note passage for the left hand in Op. 57, II, bars 64–71; the second theme of Op. 31 No. 2, I, bars 41 ff.; the right-hand *coloratura* in the Adagio of Op. 31 No. 1, bar 26.

In the fifty years since this edition first appeared its influence has been a powerful though not always a direct one.

The great editors of recent years have learned much from Schenker and have followed many of his principles in their own work. That most musicians of any cultivation have abandoned the old "practical" editions is largely due—at least indirectly—to Schenker's influence. In recent years several new *Urtext* editions of the Beethoven sonatas have appeared, including a revision of Schenker's brought out by Universal-Edition, the original publisher. Some later editors have been able to consult material unavailable to Schenker (e.g., the autographs of Opp. 53, 79 and 90). But in most important respects Schenker's edition remains superior to any other, especially in the fingerings and in reproducing Beethoven's notation. In the Henle edition, for example, the notation slur-tie-slur has been changed to a single slur with an interior tie , a change which in many cases alters the musical meaning (see comments on the fingering of Op. 81a, II, on p. viii above).

This reprint makes available to a large circle of musicians and music lovers one of the greatest achievements of twentieth-century musical scholarship. At a time like the present, when performers, theorists and musicologists carry on their work in what seems to be increasing isolation, Schenker's edition has a symbolic as well as a practical value. Its study leads one to reflect on how necessary each of these activities is to the others, and how sterile—at least in a field like music—are the results of our present-day mania for specialization. The musician who uses this edition with thought and imagination will find his efforts well repaid, for it will help him to come closer to some of the greatest music ever written.

New York — CARL SCHACHTER
July 1974

NOTE: In the headings to the sonatas, *gewidmet* = dedicated to; *Gräfin* = Countess; *Fürst* = Prince; *Baronin* = Baroness; *Graf* = Count; *Fürstin* = Princess; *Edler* = Nobleman; *komponiert im Jahre . . .* = composed in the year . . .; *Freiin* = Baroness; *Erzherzog* = Archduke.

NOTE! *Throughout the book, the measure number appears at the end of the corresponding measure.*

Preface

VORWORT

Aus Briefen Beethovens und sonstigen Äußerungen wissen wir, daß der Meister mit den Drucken seiner Werke durchaus unzufrieden gewesen ist. Sein Tadel und Zorn kam für das gedruckte Werk zu spät, nützte aber auch nicht den späteren Werken, obgleich er immer wieder darauf hinwies, daß seine Schreibart für den Inhalt wesentlich sei. Die Erstausgaben scheiterten daran, daß die Beziehung von diesem Inhalt zu dieser Schreibart nicht begriffen wurde, weil beide durchaus neuartig waren.

Beethovens Schreibart ist immer nur aus der Besonderheit der einzelnen Stelle geschöpft, so daß die Schreibart dieser Stelle auf eine andere nicht paßt. Darüber äußerte ich mich in der Erläuterungs-Ausgabe von op. 101, S. 19 wie folgt:

„Beethovens kräftiges, unmittelbares, sozusagen ton-körperliches Denken bringt ihm eine auch das Auge des Lesers sinnlich überzeugende Schreibart heran:

Das Steigen und Fallen der Linien: hier sieht man sie aus dem unteren ins obere Notensystem ziehen, dort vom oberen ins untere sinken.

Das tiefsinnige Spiel der Balken: sie künden dem Auge den Willen zur Zusammengehörigkeit hier, Trennungszwang dort.

Die geheimnisvolle Beredsamkeit der Bogen: bald fassen sie Zusammengehörendes zur Einheit oder heben deren Teile hervor, bald widersprechen sie eigens einem Zusammenhang, um das Verlangen darnach zu steigern, oft wirken sie auch gleichzeitig in verschiedener Spannweite gegeneinander.

Das Auf- und Abwärtsstreichen der Notenhälse: sie lassen uns die Töne wie gegeneinanderwirkende Schauspieler wahrnehmen, scharf umrissen im Mit- und Gegenspiel, am schönsten dort, wo z. B. ein Abwärtsstreichen lange voraus das Gegenspiel aufwärtsgestrichener Tonfolgen(oder

PREFACE

We know from Beethoven's letters and from other statements that he was not at all satisfied with the printing of his works. However, his disapproval and anger were of no use once the work had been printed. Moreover, the printing of subsequent works fared no better although he kept pointing out that his manner of notation was essential to the understanding of his musical ideas. The first editions fell short in that this connection between notation and musical ideas was not understood, both being entirely new.

Beethoven's notation always results from the particular character of the passage so that the notation of one passage is unsuitable for another. I referred to this in my annotated edition of Opus 101 (p. 19) as follows:

"In Beethoven's powerful and direct thinking tones are conceived, so to speak, as physical entities; this thinking produces for him a notation that is also perceptually convincing to the eye of the reader. The rising and falling of the lines—sometimes ascending from the lower to the upper stave, sometimes sinking from the upper to the lower. The deep significance of the beams—they convey to the eye the desire to connect or to separate. The mysterious eloquence of the slurs—sometimes they unite what belongs together or emphasize segments; sometimes they purposely contradict a connection in order to increase the desire for it, often counteracting each other simultaneously by their different time-spans. The upward or downward direction of the stems—they make us see the notes as actors in contrasting roles, clearly sketched in cooperation or counteraction; this is most beautiful when, for example, downward stemming foretells a long time ahead the counterplay of a group of notes that are stemmed up (or vice versa). The notation of the rests—they are omitted now and then in order to

AVANT-PROPOS

Nous savons par des lettres de Beethoven et par des propos qu'il a tenus à diverses reprises, que le maître était très mécontent de la façon dont furent imprimées ses œuvres. Son blâme et son courroux arrivaient trop tard pour l'impression achevée mais ne servaient même pas à améliorer celle des œuvres suivantes, malgré ses efforts à faire entendre que sa notation à lui était de la plus grande importance par rapport au contenu, à l'idée. Dans ces premières éditions on ne comprit pas la relation qui existe entre l'écriture et le contenu, parce qu'écriture et contenu étaient d'un style par trop inaccoutumé.

La notation de Beethoven est toujours issue de l'essence particulière de l'idée qu'elle exprime, de sorte que la notation de tel passage ne pourrait se rapporter indifféremment à un autre passage. J'ai dit mon opinion à ce sujet dans l'édition interprétative de l'op. 101, — à la page 19, comme suit:

»La conception forte et vigoureuse de Beethoven, sa pensée musicale immédiate, presque corporelle donnent à sa notation une facture sensiblement convaincante à l'œil:

La montée et la descente des lignes:
Ici on les voit passer de la portée inférieure à celle de dessus, — là elles retombent du haut en bas.

La disposition profondément réfléchie des barres: ici elle force l'œil à reconnaître la volition de lier, — là de séparer.

L'éloquence mystérieuse des liaisons:
Tantôt elles réunissent ce qui se tient en un tout inséparable, ou bien elles font ressortir certaines de ses parties, — tantôt elles contredisent par exprès un ensemble pour augmenter le besoin, le désir qu'on en a — souvent aussi elles agissent simultanément en se contrecarrant par une envergure différente.

L'écriture ascendante ou descendante des queues de notes:
Elle nous fait apparaître les notes comme des acteurs agissant les uns contre les autres, nettement posés dans leur jeu et contre-jeu, là surtout où la notation descendante annonce longtemps d'avance

umgekehrt) spannend ankündigt.

Das Register der Pausen: sie fehlen zuweilen, **um dem Auge das Stimmenganze luftiger zu zeigen und das Kommen und Gehen mancher Stimme nicht mehr als nötig zu unterstreichen usw."**

Nur Beethovens Schreibart kann zu seinem Inhalt führen. Jede Änderung, sei sie in bester Absicht gemacht, namentlich um auch der Menge den Zugang zu Inhalt und Vortrag zu ermöglichen, die übliche alles gleichmachende Setzerweise, die Beflissenheit, mit sogenannten Phrasierungsbogen den Inhalt zu erläutern und sonst noch Zusätze von Behelfen, die das Spiel erleichtern sollen, — alles das sperrt eher den Weg zu Beethovens Inhalt und erschwert sogar die Mechanik des Spieles! Ein Vergleich der vorliegenden Ausgabe mit sämtlichen anderen kann das Gesagte von Seite zu Seite, von Takt zu Takt erweisen.

März 1934

Heinrich Schenker, Wien

avoid emphasizing the coming and going of a part more than is necessary and in order to present the whole contrapuntal web to the reader's eye in a more transparent way."

Beethoven's notation alone can lead to an understanding of his musical ideas. Any alteration, be it made with the best intention, and especially in order to bring the musical thought closer to the public and to provide help for performance, tends rather to obstruct the access to Beethoven's compositional ideas and even makes the technique of playing more difficult! This includes standardizing the notation and attempting to "interpret" the text by means of so-called phrasing slurs and other aids intended to facilitate playing. A comparison of this edition with any other will prove the above assertion from bar to bar and from page to page.

March 1934

Heinrich Schenker, Vienna

la contre-partie d'un groupe de notes ascendantes, — ou vice-versa.

Le régistre des silences:

Ceux-ci manquent parfois pour que l'œil aie de l'ensemble des voix un aspect plus clair, plus transparent et pour que les entrées de certaines voix ou la fin de leur phrase ne soit pas soulignées inutilement, — etc.«

Seule la notation de Beethoven lui-même nous guide vers l'essence de ses œuvres. Toute modification est néfaste, fut-elle exécutée dans la meilleure intention, notamment dans celle d'ouvrir un chemin à la compréhension générale du contenu et de l'interprétation.

L'écriture habituelle avec son nivellement, — les soins employés à expliquer. à interpréter le contenu à l'aide de liaisons phraséologiques, — d'autres ajoutages tendant à faciliter le jeu, … tout ceci entrave la compréhension pour l'essence de l'œuvre de Beethoven, entrave même le mécanisme du jeu! Une comparaison entre l'édition présente et toutes les autres démontrera la vérité de ces assertions de page en page, de mesure en mesure. —

En mars 1934

Heinrich Schenker, Vienne

Ludwig van Beethoven
COMPLETE
PIANO SONATAS

Contents

Volume I

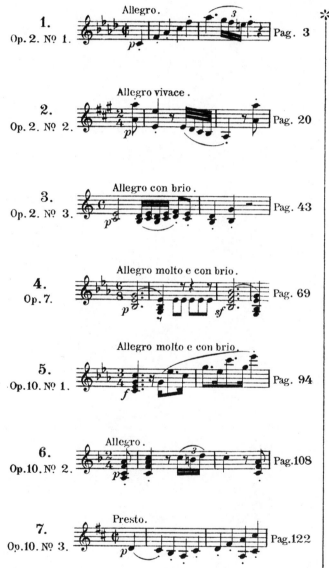

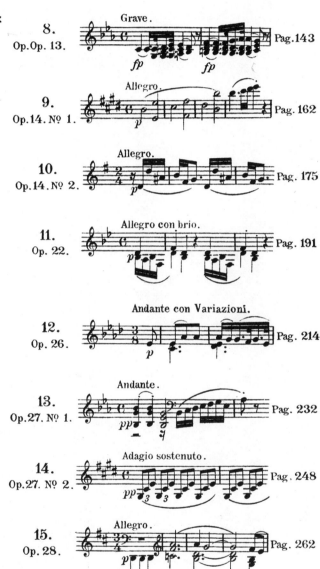

SONATE.

Op. 2. № 1.

Joseph Haydn gewidmet.

Ludwig van Beethoven.
(1770-1827.)

1) The fingering printed in italic (slanting) numbers is Beethoven's.

2) Short appoggiatura here and subsequently.

3)

4

1) d♮, not d.

1) ![figure] but in m. 44 ![figure], as in footnote 2, page 8.

MENUETTO.
Allegretto.

TRIO.

1) Expressive short appoggiatura: but cf. the written-out long appoggiatura in mm. 22 & 23.

Prestissimo.

1) or: 2) *tr* also without Nachschlag (terminating notes).

16

19

SONATE.

Op. 2. № 2.

Joseph Haydn gewidmet.

Allegro vivace.

1) The fingering in italics is Beethoven's.

1) The original Artaria edition (1796) has ∞ , Lischke's Berlin edition (1797) has ♪ .
2) Artaria has ♯♯ , Lischke has ♯ .
3) Artaria and Lischke have ♯♯ .

1) One usually plays the first 16th of each triplet with the l. h.

1) Thus in Artaria and Lischke; more recent editions have $e\flat^1$ instead of g^1.

1) Thus in Artaria
and Lischke.

26

1) Artaria and Lischke have ♮&. 2) Artaria and Lischke have #&. 3) Artaria and Lischke have &. 4) In the two earliest editions the l. h. has only
♭.
𝑒

1) For the sake of "languid expression" (C. P. E. Bach), the turn may be played already on the second 8th-beat.

1) The trill begins on the main note; it is
   sufficient to play it in 32nds.

2) The trill begins from below (in 32nds) on the third
   quarter-beat.

3) To be played as in m. 9.

4) As in m. 7.

5)

1) L. h. notation as in Artaria; Lischke has merely and more recent editions have:

SCHERZO.
Allegretto.

1) Expressive short appoggiatura.

Fine.

TRIO.

Scherzo D. C.

RONDO.
Grazioso.

1) **ff** as in Lischke; Artaria places it in the preceding measure.

34

1) The 16th $c\sharp^2$ may be shortened to a 32nd.

1) Actually a turn between 2 notes; the final note has been written in full size in its proper position.

40

SONATE.

Op. 2. No 3.

Joseph Haydn gewidmet.

1) The fingering in italics is Beethoven's.

1) *(musical example)*   2) Without Nachschlag.

1) Short appoggiatura:

1) To be played as in mm. 45 & 46.

53

56

SCHERZO.
Allegro.

1) The trill also with a short appoggiatura:

58

TRIO.

Allegro assai.

64

SONATE.

Op. 7.

Der Gräfin Babette von Keglevics gewidmet.

Allegro molto e con brio.

70

1) Contrary to the original edition, Artaria 1797, most editions print at this place the chromatic e♮ (before the e♭); but here the composition does not imitate the chromatic middle voice of mm. 63–65; rather it prepares for the diatonic one of mm. 73 & 74.

1) The first edition lacks the ♮ before the g^1, but $g♭$ is needed here because of the mixture that follows.

76

1) Cf. the remark on m. 72.

78

1) Here the l. h. plays over the r. h.

Largo, con gran espressione.

81

1) Thus in the first edition; more recent editions have *ab* only on the 3rd quarter-beat.

82

1) Here the last note of the turn has been written in full size, a correct notation often used by the old masters.

Allegro D.C.

RONDO.
Poco allegretto e grazioso.

1) It is sufficient to play the shortest trill of 5 notes beginning with the main note (see the fingering).

2) Thus in the original edition; several editors changed this passage in analogy to mm. 135–139, thus introducing a g³ impossible on Beethoven's piano.

1) See footnote to m. 42.

SONATE.

Op. 10. № 1

Der Gräfin von Browne gewidmet.

Allegro molto e con brio.

1) [musical example] and thus in mm. 3, 9, 11, etc. 2) [musical example] 3) Perhaps: [musical example] 4) The whole run is to be played on the fourth 16th-beat.

1) The turn is to be played before the *c♭''*, so that that note receives its full 32nd value.

2)

3) *a♭* in the autograph presumably tied to next measure.

FINALE.
Prestissimo

1) Thus in the original edition; a later edition gives:

SONATE

Op.10. Nº 2.

Der Gräfin von Browne gewidmet.

1) The turn is to be played before the $c\sharp$, so that that note receives its full 16th value.

1) The practice in recent editions of making this group analogous to the figure of the second quarter-beat in m. 98, giving

is unacceptable, since Beethoven's tone sense would not have permitted the single occurrence of such a high note (bb^3) in the course of a movement even if the note had been available to him.

112

Allegretto.

1) Expressive short appoggiatura: 2) ***p*** as in the original edition, Eder 1798.   3)

118

120

SONATE.

Op. 10. № 3.

Der Gräfin von Browne gewidmet.

1) The fingering in italics is Beethoven's. 2) The octaves are lacking here in the original edition, Eder 1798. They are given in the later editions, although this makes performance unnecessarily difficult. 3) Beethoven's piano reached only up to f^3.

1) Short appoggiatura.

1) In more recent editions, the octave leaps are carried up to a^3. 2) The original edition lacks the tie in the l. h. here and in m. 286.

1) In the original edition the next *sf* is reserved for the chord in m. 183. 2) Recent editions have octaves from this point.

65

MENUETTO.
Allegro.

Fine.

138

RONDO.
Allegro.

1) Short appoggiatura.

SONATE. (PATHÉTIQUE.)
Op. 13.
Dem Fürsten Carl von Lichnowsky gewidmet.

L. v. Beethoven.

Attacca subito l' Allegro:

1) Three triplets. 2) Here 6 = 3 x 2. 3) Here 6 = 2 x 3.

1) Short appoggiatura.

Interlude

Tempo I.

Allegro molto e con brio.

148

RONDO.
Allegro.

1)

2) Short appoggiatura.

159

SONATE

Op.14. No.1.

Der Baronin von Braun gewidmet.

1) *i.e. the turn should be played within the first 8th-beat.*

2) The l. h. plays the lowest note of the chord.

165

1) Thus in the original Mollo and Simrock editions; recent editions make this analogous to mm. 44 & 45, which, however, could not be played on Beethoven's piano.

RONDO.
Allegro comodo.

SONATE.
Op.14, No 2.
Der Baronin von Braun gewidmet.

1) Short appoggiatura. 2) The turn is to be played in the preceding measure.

1) Thus in the original Mollo and Simrock editions; recent editions make this analogous to m. 170, which, however, could not be played on Beethoven's piano.

1) Thus in the original editions; recent editions have ♮ as in m. 4; see footnote to m. 43.

Andante.
La prima parte senza replica.

65
p
decresc.
pp
p
sempre legato
cresc.
70
rinf.
cresc.
rinf.
p
p
75
p
cresc.
p
cresc.
80
(cresc.)
sf
sf

SCHERZO.
Allegro assai.

1) Short appoggiatura.

SONATE.
Op. 22.
Dem Grafen von Browne gewidmet.

Allegro con brio.

1) c^3 in the revised copy too, not bb^2 as in many editions.

1) Thus also in the revised copy, in contrast to m. 43.

199

1) Short appoggiatura. 2) The turn, with ♭♮ and ♮, is to be played on the second 16th-beat of the second 8th-beat.

1) The turn is to be played before the 16th bb^1.

RONDO.
Allegretto.

1) [music example]

2) The turn is to be played before the dotted 16th c^2.

1) Recent editions make an analogy with m. 33, but an octave higher.

2) With Nachschlag.

213

Sonate

Op. 26.

Dem Fürsten Carl von Lichnowsky gewidmet

L. van Beethoven

Andante con Variazioni.

1) The pedal indications are Beethoven's.
2) Short appoggiatura.

Var. I.

1) Execute as in m. 25 of the Theme.

Var. II.

218

1) Thus in the autograph; in the original edition (Cappi) mistakenly: etc.

221

SCHERZO. La prima parte senza repetitione.
Allegro molto.

1) In m. 46 and likewise m. 54 the autograph does not have the ♮ signs; the original edition shows them, in conflict with the A♭-major harmony which binds the whole passage together.

Scherzo da capo
senza repetizione.

1) In order to clearly contrast the new rhythm 𝅗𝅥. with the rhythm of the upper voice in mm. 68–87, 𝅗𝅥 𝅘𝅥, Beethoven writes here: The original edition gives this passage without the ties: 𝆑 etc.

MARCIA FUNEBRE sulla morte d'un eroe.

SONATE.

Op. 27. № 1.

(Sonata quasi una Fantasia.)

Der Fürstin von Liechtenstein gewidmet.

1) In the original edition (Cappi) the fingering is 3.

1

Attacca subito l'Allegro.

Allegro molto vivace.

1) Trill with Nachschlag.

237

Attacca subito V Adagio.

Adagio con espressione.

Attacca subito l'Allegro vivace.

Allegro vivace.

1) The l. h. over the r. h. 2) The l. h. below the r. h.

245

1) The l. h over the r. h. 2) The l. h. below the r. h. 3) L. h. above. 4) L. h. below.

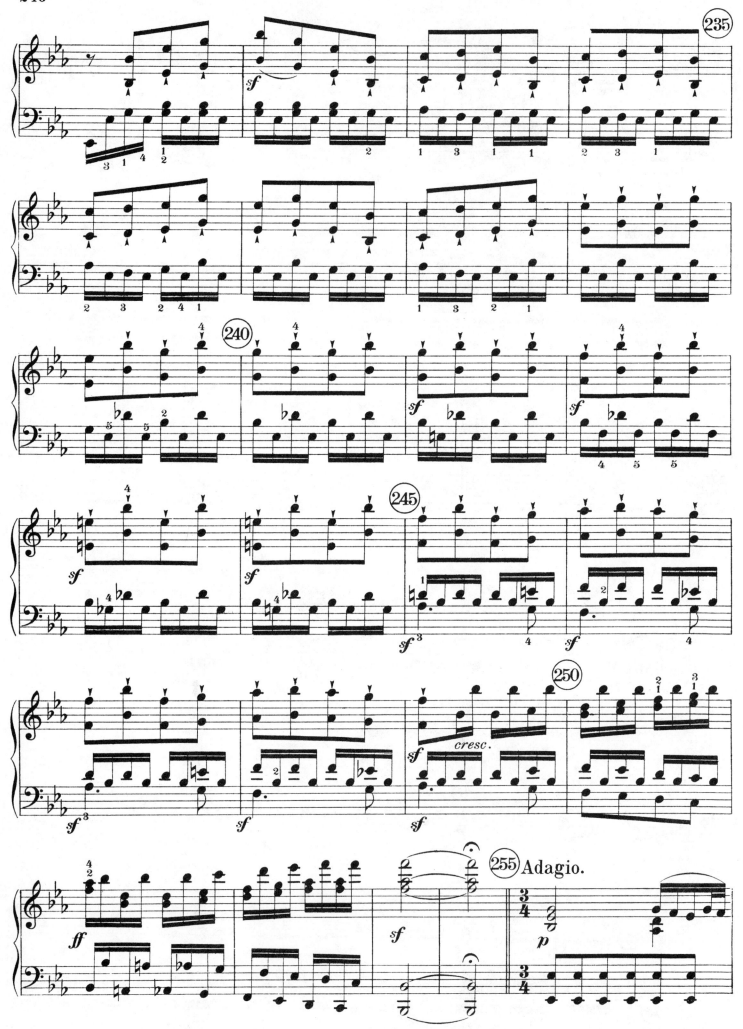

SONATE.

Op.27. Nº 2.

(Sonata quasi una Fantasia.)

Der Gräfin Julie Guicciardi gewidmet.

Adagio sostenuto.

Si deve suonare tutto questo pezzo delicatissimamente e senza sordini.

14.

sempre pianissimo e senza sordini

1) The pedal indications are Beethoven's.

Attacca subito il seguente.

Allegretto.
La prima parte senza repetizione.

TRIO.

Fine.

Allegretto da capo.

Presto agitato.

255

SONATE.

Op. 28.

Joseph Edlen von Sonnenfels gewidmet.

Komponiert im Jahre 1801.

NOTE! All the printed measure numbers in this movement should be increased by 1 (i.e. the measure marked 5 is actually measure 6, etc.).

Allegro.

15.

1) The fingering in italics and the pedal indications are Beethoven's.

1) In this passage and the corresponding one in the recapitulation, the autograph does not show slurs, although they appear in the original edition.

1) No slurs here either in the autograph or the original edition.

265

266

1) The original fingerings come from F. Starke's *Wiener Pianoforteschule*, 1820, to which Beethoven contributed the Andante (abridged) and the Rondo.

SCHERZO.
Allegro vivace.

Fine.

TRIO.

La seconda parte una volta

Scherzo da capo.

RONDO.
Allegro ma non troppo.

1) Short appoggiatura.

Episode - a notive that is
developmental going through
different keys (new idea)

interlude - something not expected
repeat of something known.

Episode - a notive that is
developmental going through
different keys (new idea)

interlude - something not expected
repeat of something known.